The Uniform Factory
Louise Fazackerley

VERVE
POETRY PRESS
BIRMINGHAM

PUBLISHED BY VERVE POETRY PRESS
https://vervepoetrypress.com
mail@vervepoetrypress.com

The right of Louise Fazackerley to be identified as author of this work has been asserted in accordance with section 77 of the Copyright, Designs and Patents Act 1988.

FIRST PUBLISHED SEP 2020

Printed and bound in the UK
by Positive Print, Birmingham

ISBN: 978-1-912565-41-2

Cover Artwork Credit: Jim Winters

CONTENTS

Acknowledgements

*for Daniel
and Uncle Maurice*

The Uniform Factory

Passing Out Parade (1998)

If this were a wedding picture
you'd be marrying your Dad.
Centre-stage, his hair like a yard-brush,
his tash like a prison officer's.
Chief-bridesmaid; your poor Mam,
the awkward angles of her crap blue suit.
I see you managed to get your Craig
out of The Oak, right wing
our Katie is meek, verdant and mute.
Down-stage left, Barbie-ex stands
in my place-to-be. Big-jugged and bright,
she's on her way out, the great escape.
Your face, narrow as pointing,
peaked cap jammed on.
I can't see your eyes. I don't know you, yet.
Your backwards family all face forward.
      Peg dolls- the lot of you.

Another Place

I pack the car for Crosby Beach,   *again?*
You shower, shaving sideburns, high and tight.
I shove cracked buckets, spades and blankets in.
You, wind   the bow-shaped bobbin of the kite.
Our girls run fast enough to fall *just cry*
or fly like swallows.   You are *late* to shore.
Your dumb speech, foam. We do not touch at all.
In all, we are not lovers anymore.
Another man holds your daughter's hand,
brass faced *no* looking out to sea,
like sentries looking for a place to *please.*
The sand black bruise the broken boat.
King's Shilling spent. Small honour and obey.
For now, you're standing, still, we walk away.

factory

staple shaped table shaped
bucket shaped they try to fill us
well? well? unwell
shoulder pads in blazers
like polypropylene dimples stacked
we are lined paper
screamed at
matchbox
chair on two legs
middle finger
both hands
everyone knows
they look like prisons
they shut us down
they shut us
they

all that's left is
this, sir

uniform

sold yer hoodie *sold yer* no mark *sold yer* hoodwinked *sold yer* no chance
sold yer no brand *sold yer* trackies *sold yer* sport *sold yer* no chance
sold yer trainers *sold yer* train me *soldier* trainee *sold yer* no chance

Landay

The drones have come to a British sky
The mouths of our rockets will sound in reply

Street Life

Let me show you how we live.
A Pac-Man maze of terraced streets,
built 1906. Back-to-backs in Accrington brick
and souped-up cars with neon lights
like flying saucers; they bass, vibrate, *fucking fly*!
Dot-to-dot a buzzing perimeter,
the invisible electric fence
keeps the sheep, the wolves,
the smiley faces and ghosts
all in it together. We're all in it together.

Yet despite cheap water, cheap
Council Tax, cheap strangers don't buy
houses here. No matter how fecund
of thought they are. No matter
how many crackled *cast iron-baths*
and other original features survive?

Purring clogs to Nike mufflers,
coal-dust to spray-on skins,
skint. *Let them tan!*
Let them eat cake, pies and KFC!
To a soundtrack of Grand Theft Auto,
where rev and rips race - no helmets on -
on a patchwork track of cobbles,
tarmac and threadbare grass.
There's still some cobbles here.
                              Picturesque.

Motorbility scooters race.
They scribble round cars
piled on kerbs, old cars stacked
against houses, like a topple of dominoes.
Anyone for a game of 5's and 3's?
   Does no-one go to work on this street?
There's no parking spaces, no walking spaces
on my terraced row
and the pavements are tight.

Let me show you how we live.
The dogs, the dogs are muscular
like meathead masters,
or the dogs are muscular
and their masters are frail, old
with sticks and you hope
the dog is under control
Does he bite, mister??
Wheel the pram across the road.

Or dogs, muscular with half-light masters
who are thin, off their heads,
prescription meds, booze,
the walking dead, the Resident Evil,
Ey love, have you got a light?
Young, soft-lads snigger, under control,
Brrap, Brrap
  I know what I'll be doing
when the zombie apocolypse comes.
And this is a career plan.

the working men's club in the street next door
has an act on, and the children dream
in 1980's golden spool.

Shut all your windows.
Turn the telly right up.
You can just about escape
a Sunday care home singalong.
The residents shuffle across to the club -

> *It's a long way for half a shandy,*
> *it's a long way to go,*
> *without your carer*

> *Pack up your troubles*
> *in your oxygen tank*
> *and smile, smile, smile*

Let me show you how we die.
Amongst council castles,
high rise mansions
and rounds of ammunition.
Trigger-happy toddlers
tapping touchscreen phones,
kids on consoles- Call of Duty.
Lads, girls and men,
climb derelict buildings and
swing on ropes across the cut.
We fight; girl on girl,
boy on boy, girl on boy.

Little adrenaline junkies-
already started Basic Training,

Phase Zero,
zero else to do,
but brainwashing, recession,
economic conscription
(the music starts up
Chopin's Funeral March
- a big screen version)
Duh, duh, duh, duh, duh, duh
Slates begin to fall as roofs peel back
and the ground is shaking, something inside cracks
as rising from the earth,
the interior of these measly dwellings
shiny tipped projectiles emerge,
brown belt of bullets,
a row of little metal teeth,
a fox trap, *tally ho boys,*
orange brick dust obfuscates like gunpowder
poverty is the primer
like a Tornado in the desert and all that sand, sand,
like dried faeces *just blowing in the wind*
of all those third world countries you're going to visit
Join the Army. Travel the world.
like the turning of an hour glass
like the turning of an hour glass
like the turning of an hour glass

bang

Front Line

Jumping Jaks on King St.
I'm a sniper.

> Kerpink, pink, pink shots
> in a sticky-out party dress.

His t-shirt
a target on the front.

Wallflower. I pick him.

He never stood a chance.

What do you do?
I'm a secret agent.

Only Bolton could take a bullet to the head and still not be dead
Medic! Medic!

He's a medic, and a medic is not allowed to fire his weapon
unless he's being fired upon,

they just traipse round after the infantry
half a man, waiting for someone to step on a bomb.

Don't worry, lad. You'll discharge your weapon
before the end of this tour.

No- they don't just press a button

missile flies
pixelated pictures
on a flat screen TV
die

Oh, turn it over love.

the front line is there
the front line is here.

Souvenir

sandswept by him
I'm debris

  whirlpool

driftwood
I'm on your side

still babies unsqualling

anchor

stormed into blue eyes
sucked in

Daddy's boat

she makes you a little boat
a margarine tub, an orange paper sail
I can't fold into a B.F.P.O email

you miss her first day of school
you miss her nativity play
six months tour, your theatre is war

you ring insecure on an unsecured line
I witter on- house, kids, work
omitting drinks with a male friend
paranoid thoughts, another insurgent

your letters bleed, a sleepless hell
sniper shots, hobbled little boys
patch them up and send them on
to guns

I can't think straight

the things you learn while she learns
what you destroy while she creates

I'm almost
hating you,
the army,
this world

shake myself, get a grip
there must be more to life than this

with a bright idea and a bit of hope
I take this childish, fragile boat

get a shoebox to send to Afghanistan
tissue paper crumpled in
I can't let you sink,
I need you to swim

put all your death-long days
the loneliness and all the scary stuff
into this boat she made for you
the love should stop it seeping through

somebody stop this happening to us
somebody stop this happening to me

when you come home we'll launch that boat
you and I will be free

Landay

You're home and everything is perfect
Paroxetine can make an erection last for hours

Weather Report

we're the snow-globe in summer
we're sand-globe in winter

at night the temperature drops
I curl round him to keep him warm
he's like a corpse, there's no response

it's cluttered in here,
headfuck head-shaped dome
unwanted gift from his little trip abroad

the turn of, the night and day of
a glass tent, glass spherical
Standard Army issue-
they give them to soldiers
like soldiers throwing sweets to kids

Afghanistan
like nowhere else in the world
he sleeps with his boots on and shakes like a feral dog

call it doll's house, call it fish tank, call it HOME SWEET HOME
it's cluttered in here with broken things
stupid

a limb has bent at the elbow
punched a light socket in the front room
the crack in the plastic is the shape of lightening

when a mine shaft collapses
it leaves the same shape in the earth
as a punch in a chipboard door

the baby gate thrown down the stairs
the golf clubs wrapped round trees
the window put through- glass to glass

ashes to ashes, dust to dust
his throat's so dry,
he has to have a drink with all the—
A man can have a drink in his own house, can't he?
Int that what we were fighting for?

... there's bit of him under my fingernails
and I'm washing my hands, I'm washing my
hands, I'm washing my hands
and Bolton comes over,
he can see I'm struggling.
He brings this big bottle of water and he pours

I can't open the door
in case the nightmares fly out
I can't open the door
in case someone hears him
I can't open the door
in case the sand pours out
and makes a road block
and no-one can get to work
and people sink in it and go under

I can't open the door
because of all the blood

we're sort of safe in this glass house
just watching, our faces pressed against the pane
as you, as you, as you walk past

we're the snow-globe in summer
we're the sand-globe in winter

Landay

Be iodine-yellow or blood-red
but don't come home whole and disgrace my bed

Bolton's Party – (a response to Kipling's Recessional)

It was after the inquest, at the pub—
When we meet Private Bolton's mum—
We drink to wash away the blood
And joke he'd wish that he had come.
She grabs your hand, don't go yet,
Lest we forget—lest we forget!

She's Brasso- tries to make nowt nice—
She tells us Bolton's latest post—
She hears him in the house at night
And laughs to hear her lost son's ghost
She grabs your hand, don't leave us yet,
Lest we forget—lest we forget!

Each year we're summoned to his house

It's like he's nipped out for a cig
A squaddie do. Pints, shots and Scouse.
In smoke, she sees the shape of him.
It's almost like, he's not gone yet
Lest we forget—lest we forget!

'Happy Birthday, Bolton, lad'
They ask you why you left.
'Coz the Army's sent me fucking mad
—Give it a fucking rest.'
I grab your hand, we can't go yet
Lest we forget—lest we forget!

Three years on, the party's bare
Uncomfortable, we understand
I ask her if his ghost's still there
'No, love,' she says with shaking hands.
No monument to him. No parties anymore.

When we forget, can we move on?

Who's all this fighting for?

Landay

Our leaders burn fields of pacifists
Sir. Stone them. Those who control the jobs control the world

Remembrance Someday

ticktockticktock

See the sterile clock with it's can-can legs,
the frou-frou ticking of the red second hand,
no, the third hand, seconds are amputated,
only 3 fingers, a capital letter T. Tut tut tut.
Time disagrees with your use of it.

It clicks as a horse clops,
as the plack plack of the princess shoes
of a child on laminate floor.
Shhhh. Be quiet. Daddy's in bed.
Daddy's been asleep for a long time.

Jam a pen in the march of that clock
and turn it, turn it. Turn it forwards,

wait, Daddy's in the bath.
Body temperature, where blood
like egg yolk flowers
in bathwater.

The poppy, dropped on blue lino
at the side of the bath.

A prick of the pin, a rake of the knife,
that plastic green stem is whirring round
and round, tickticktick,, twitching, defibrillating,

the raw red paper of helicopter blades
begin to hum and roar- men scream in relief,
an hours wait, *the morphine's wearing off*,
this man, *this boy is still alive*, handover to the doctors,
they can fly away without jumping

from the white of the bath like the white of the
ward like the white of the eyes of one, two,
one, two, one, two, one, two, three boys
who you saved, who were supposed to survive,
like the white of the poppy the pacifist wears
like the white of your anger, like the white
shrouds of Afghan dead, like the dirty, white
of my wedding vows, like the white teeth
of Azad, haggling for chickens,
like the white of the fallen feathers, like the
white of divorce papers in the shredder,
like the white of the skirting boards
you scrub and scrub, like the white of the
toothpaste on your daughter's cheek
like the white bone of the domino

Clock face. About turn. *Left march*.
Remembrance Sunday.
A service, a cenotaph, Ince shopping precinct.

watched by William Hill and Nisa,
watched by Tattoos by Lisa,
watched by the Colonol, you know, the KFC.

The kids made bucketful
of the clots, at school.
Mummy, look!
She wears it as a garland.

You won't wear your medals.

a spattering of soldiers,
old, old soldiers,
their spines curve,
the ramrod frames of them
sink into the earth,
bodies, mud dolls,
skin trying to fall from faces like
red roads of leaves, aching with gravity,
like dry, yellow leaves, aching with poverty

a meme echoing round my skull
fight for your world, not for your country
fight for your world, not for your country

You? You're sort of timeless.
You're still, somehow, away,
I try to catch your eye.

No eye contact with the enemy.

Umbilical height,
buds of opium nod like shaven heads.
You're dreaming of marching at night,
waist-high in stinking water
irrigated melon fields, chains grow
like Christmas baubles,and incendiary devices
the dog didn't find it
the metal detectors didn't find it

the inside is red and wet
painting the sand like a Pollock
and you're scrubbing your hands, you're scrubbing

Fast forward.
I'm warm, sat in a flat at the top of the high-rises
with my great-uncle Patrick, bedbound
and the view of this Northern town
of canals, industrial estates
and mossed over mineshafts

Our Pat tells me about his Dad,
glad to join up at 17,
NO BLACKS NO DOGS NO IRISH
no work for us
great-Grandad Collins, prisoner of war for six months
six months tour, your theatre is war
in Mesopotania, or, nowadays- Iraq.

Something inside me cracks,

Iraqi women encircling British soldiers
to stop their husbands from killing them, in 1906
something inside me cracks,
while the CO *that's Commanding Officer to you*
while the CO welcomes them back in 1907 with
Oh, my poor boys, my poor, poor boys.

Will we never hear the end of it?
John Joseph, drinking father,
playing squeezebox carols
for booze round all the local pubs,
the melodium, Mesopotania,
and an old man's tears at an old, old story.

That green plastic needle on the gramophone
keeps hicupping, keeps hopping, keeps jumping,
the same story again and again
a broken, red record, round and round.

Remembrance Some Day.
This little plastic and paper poppy burns,
passed down and down.

Why do we remember, but never seem to learn?
And you're washing your hands, you're washing your hands,
you're washing your hands.

ACKNOWLEDGEMENTS

The first incarnation of this pamphlet existed as a piece of performance written for the BBC Radio 3 New Voices award, in collaboration with New Writing North, BBC Radio 3, Arc-Stockton, Contact-Manchester and The Writers Squad. The 20 minute performance of dance and poetry or 'high theatre' was called 'Love Is A Battlefield.' Thanks to Lee Affen for under-scoring the piece with such haunting music, to dance artist Giorgio Deca for choreography and performance, to Matt Fenton and Peader Kirk for directing and to the team at BBC Radio 3 'The Verb' for your support, broadcasting and encouragement, especially Ian McMillan.

The second coming of this pamphlet can be heard in the audiobook 'Council House Poetry' published by Nymphs & Thugs and shortlisted for a Saboteur Award for 'Best Spoken Word Show' after a run at the Edinburgh Fringe. Thanks to Matt Abbott for total belief in me and my work.

This final version, born as 'The Uniform Factory,' gestated during my MA in Creative Writing at Edge Hill University. It includes some landays. Landays are a two line poetic form written and sung by Pshtun women on the Pakistan/Afghanistan border. It is traditional to pass landays from woman to woman and then re-work them as your own. I was introduced to landays via an article by Eliza Griswold on the Poetry Foundation website. I urge you to read it and watch the film made by Seamus Murphy to find out more about the position of women writing poetry in rural Afghanistan. At time of press I am working to make connections and opportunities with and for Pashtun poets in the UK. Thanks to Stuart Bartholomew at Verve Poetry Press for his patience and vision.

ABOUT THE AUTHOR

Poet-extraordinaire, educator and luminary, Louise Fazackerley writes
darkly humorous, working class narratives of hope and hurt. She
has two collections published with Verve Poetry Press, 'The Lolitas'
and 'The Uniform Factory.' One collection published with The Secret
Writers Club- 'Bird St.' and an audio-book 'Council House Poetry'
published with Nymphs & Thugs. Louise lives with her two teenage
daughters in Wigan and two cats called Ginny and Vivienne.

website: www.louisethepoet.co.uk
social media: @louisethepoet

ABOUT VERVE POETRY PRESS

Verve Poetry Press is a fairly new and already award-winning press focussied initially on meeting a need in Birmingham - a need for the vibrant poetry scene here in Brum to find a way to present itself to the poetry world via publication. Co-founded by Stuart Bartholomew and Amerah Saleh, it is publishing poets from all corners of the city - poets that represent the city's varied and energetic qualities and will communicate its many poetic stories.

Added to this is a colourful pamphlet series featuring poets who have previously performed at our sister festival - and a poetry show series which captures the magic of longer poetry performance pieces by poets such as Polarbear and Matt Abbott.

Like the festival, we will strive to think about poetry in inclusive ways and embrace the multiplicity of approaches towards this glorious art.

In 2019 the press was voted Most Innovative Publisher at the Saboteur Awards, and won the Publisher's Award for Poetry Pamphlets at the Michael Marks Awards.

www.vervepoetrypress.com
@VervePoetryPres
mail@vervepoetrypress.com